JAN 1 3 2005

W9-BAG-229

Theodore Roosevelt

Theodore Roosevelt

Sean McCollum

AMERICA'S
26TH
PRESIDENT

Children's Press®
A Division of Scholastic Inc.
New York / Toronto / London / Auckland / Sydney
Mexico City / New Delhi / Hong Kong
Danbury, Connecticut

Library of Congress Cataloging-in-Publication Data

McCollum, Sean.
    Theodore Roosevelt / by Sean McCollum.
        v. cm. — (Encyclopedia of presidents. Second series)
        Includes bibliographical references and index.
Contents: Mind and body—Triumphs and tragedies—The rough rider—A man
of destiny—Finale—The uses of power
    ISBN 0-516-22964-8
        1. Roosevelt, Theodore, 1858–1919—Juvenile literature. 2. Presidents—
United States—Biography—Juvenile literature. [1. Roosevelt, Theodore,
1858–1919. 2. Presidents.] I. Title. II. Series.
E757.M447 2004
973.91'1'092—dc22   2003027884

Contents

Chapter 1

"The Great Day of My Life" —————

At the foot of San Juan Heights, U.S. soldiers are taking heavy fire. Bullets from Spanish sharpshooters on the hilltops whip through the grass, making a "chug" sound when they smack flesh. The nearby creek turns red as the blood of dead, dying, and wounded men flows into it.

A stocky, thick-necked officer shifts impatiently among his troops, his spectacles flashing, white teeth snapping. Where is the order to advance? Finally, the command comes. Colonel Theodore Roosevelt swings onto his horse, Little Texas. He urges his troops, his "Rough Riders," up Kettle Hill. When one trooper hesitates to rise from his hiding place, Roosevelt scolds him: "Are you afraid to stand up when I am on horseback?" That instant, the man is struck by a bullet, but Roosevelt rides on.

Theodore Roosevelt (center) with his Rough Riders in Cuba, soon after they captured Kettle Hill in 1898. Roosevelt considered the battle the high point of his life.

As the charge continues, other units join. A bullet grazes Roosevelt's elbow. He comes to a fence and is forced to leave his horse behind. He joins his men at a trot. The enemy rises up to meet them. The Americans do not stop. Spanish soldiers fall, and their comrades retreat. The Rough Riders charge to the top of Kettle Hill. Soon afterward, they join in the storming of neighboring San Juan Hill. The stunned Spanish soldiers fall back toward the town of Santiago.

The battle is won, and Theodore Roosevelt has passed his own ultimate test of personal courage. His well-publicized role in the victory will help propel him to the highest public office in the United States. But for today, leading and fighting is enough.

During his life, Roosevelt gained recognition as a naturalist, public official, rancher, family man, big-game hunter, and president of the United States. He threw himself into enough adventures for ten lifetimes. Tackling challenges and refusing to shrink from danger were hallmarks of his life. "Teddy is consumed with energy as long as he is doing something and fighting somebody," said his friend Cecil Spring Rice. "He always finds something to do and somebody to fight."

Yet after all his lifetime achievements—even his eventful years as president—nothing ever matched that battlefield charge on July 1, 1898. Near the end of his life, Roosevelt said, "San Juan was the great day of my life."

The Sickly Naturalist

It's a wonder that Theodore Roosevelt accomplished much at all. "Teedie," as he was called, was born on October 27, 1858, in the heart of New York City. He was the second of four children and the eldest son of Theodore Roosevelt Sr. and Martha Bulloch Roosevelt. From an early age, he was a sickly child, often tormented by asthma. "One of my memories," he recalled in his autobiography, "is

"Teedie" at about six years old.

of my father walking me up and down in the room in his arms at night when I was a very small person and of sitting up in bed gasping, with my father and mother trying to help me."

The family was among the wealthiest and best known in the city. Real estate deals had created a family fortune. This allowed Teedie's millionaire father to spend much of his time promoting charity work—raising money for orphanages, children's hospitals, and other causes. He sometimes brought his children along to volunteer at these projects.

In spite of his asthma, young Teedie was a lively child. "He is brimming full of mischief

The "Roosevelt Museum of Natural History"

Throughout his life, Theodore Roosevelt had a passion for *natural history*, especially the study of animals. He made constant notes about what he saw, and at age nine wrote his first effort at a book, which he called "Natural History of Insects."

Live specimens from his "Roosevelt Museum of Natural History" sometimes escaped his room. Visitors learned to check the water pitcher for snakes and the couch cushions for escaped creatures. He also studied animals in the wild, becoming an expert at identifying birds by sight and sound.

At age twelve Theodore got his first gun, and his love affair with hunting began. In those days students of animal life often hunted and killed interesting animals, then studied their bodies. Theodore taught himself the art of taxidermy (the stuffing of dead animals) so that he could preserve his specimens. He often reeked of dead creatures and taxidermists' chemicals. Many of the exotic animals he hunted later in his life were stuffed and displayed at leading natural history museums.

☆ ★ ☆

and has to be watched all the time," wrote his mother when he was three. By age seven, he filled his days with playmates, exploration, games, books, and animals. He began to collect every creature he could capture. With help from his cousins, he set up the "Roosevelt Museum of Natural History" in his bedroom.

One day before he turned twelve, his father sat him down for a talk. Teedie's older sister Anna, called "Bamie," recalled the conversation. "Theodore," his father said, "you have the mind but you have not the body, and without the help of the body the mind cannot go as far as it should. You must make your body. It is hard drudgery to make one's body, but I know you will do it."

"I'll make my body," the boy answered.

The family installed gym equipment on the second floor. There, the boy lifted weights, boxed, and practiced tumbling and gymnastics. Gradually, Theodore gained strength, stamina, and confidence, and the asthma attacks became fewer and farther between. True to his father's words, his body no longer limited his already muscular mind.

Up to this time, Theodore had received little regular schooling. An aunt, Annie Bulloch, had tutored him off and on, and Theodore showed flashes of brilliance in reading and writing. Spelling was a problem, though, and math would always be a challenge for him. When he turned 15, his education took on a new urgency. His father expected him to enroll at Harvard College in a few years, and he needed to catch up. A private tutor named Arthur Cutler was engaged to work with Theodore, his brother Elliott, and a cousin. Cutler found Theodore an active and energetic student. "The young man never seemed to know what idleness was," the teacher recalled, "and every leisure moment would find the last novel, some English classic or some abstruse book on Natural History in his hands."

Theodore at age 17 (standing at left) with his sister Corinne (center) and brother Elliott. Sitting on the ground is a friend, Edith Carow, who later became Roosevelt's second wife.

Theodore passed the Harvard entrance exams with high marks. In 1876, he left New York City behind for new challenges as a scholar in Cambridge, Massachusetts.

An Eccentric at Harvard

Theodore was an odd freshman at Harvard College in 1876 and did not fit in easily. The student style at the time was to act bored and world-weary. Theodore was too passionate about life to mask his energy and enthusiasm. "It was not considered good form to move at more than a walk," remembered one classmate. "Roosevelt was always running." He filled his small apartment with stuffed birds and crawling reptiles.

His intelligence and abilities were never in question, and he soon proved to be an above-average student, helped by an amazing memory. Later as president, he would amaze friends by reciting long poems he had not read in years. He also had intense powers of concentration. Once while reading by a fireplace, he became so lost in a book that he didn't notice that his boots were smoking.

Gradually, Theodore transformed himself into a dandy. He wore fancy suits, sported a walking stick, and (following the day's fashion) parted his hair in the middle. He also grew stylish side-whiskers, which gave him the appearance of a chipmunk with its cheeks full of nuts. In class, his inquiring mind spurred him

The Boxer

When Theodore was 13, two bullies harassed him. When he tried to fight back, they toyed with him and teased him. To prevent a repeat of that humiliation, he took up boxing. He lacked natural talent, but his relentless practice honed his fighting skills. During his junior year at Harvard he fought for the school's title as a 135-pound lightweight. It was soon clear that Theodore was no match for the defending champ, C. S. Hanks, but he demonstrated his dogged determination. "It was no fight at all," a spectator commented. "You should have seen that little fellow staggering about, banging the air. Hanks couldn't put him out and Roosevelt wouldn't give up. It wasn't a fight, but, oh, he showed himself a fighter!"

☆ ★ ☆

to question and argue. He sometimes jumped to his feet to challenge his instructors. After one long harangue, an exasperated professor interrupted him, saying, "See here, Roosevelt, let me talk. I'm running this course."

Roosevelt pursued his interest in natural sciences and considered making a career in the field. His father respected this, but warned Theodore that he must pursue it seriously and not as a rich man's hobby. In February 1878, during his second year at Harvard, Theodore lost this rock of support and good advice. His father died of cancer at age 46, battering 19-year-old Theodore with grief.

The memory of his father continued to influence Theodore Jr. throughout his life. His younger sister, Corinne, recalled years later, "When the college boy of 1878 was entering upon his duties as president of the United States, he told me frequently that he never took any serious step or made any vital decision for his country without thinking first what position his father would have taken on the question."

Theodore in Love

During his third year at Harvard, Roosevelt fell in love. Alice Hathaway Lee was the cousin of a classmate, a tall 17-year-old with striking blue-gray eyes, blond curls, and the ready smile that won her the nickname "Sunshine." She found him interesting but odd, just as capable of pulling a dead animal out of his pocket as paying her a compliment.

With his irrepressible style, he set about wooing her. "See that girl?" he is reported to have told a friend, pointing out Alice at a party. "I am going to marry her. She won't have me, but I'm going to have her." When Theodore proposed marriage to Alice, she refused. Before long, however, he mounted another campaign to win her hand. When he proposed a second time, in January 1880, Alice agreed. The date was set for fall 1880, on October 27, his birthday.

That spring, Theodore graduated from Harvard with honors, ranking 21st in his class of 177. His interest in a scientific career had faded, and he had taken increased interest in government and history. He never lost his love of natural history, but he would gain his fame in other fields.

Chapter 2

Law and Politics

Roosevelt returned to New York City in the fall of 1880 and enrolled at the Columbia University Law School. In October, he and Alice were married in Brookline, Massachusetts. He was 22 and Alice was 19.

Roosevelt was blissfully happy with Alice, but he was less happy with his studies. He found the detailed, plodding study of the law boring. He soon discovered that activities at the 21st District Republican Association, the local party headquarters, were much more his style, and there he began his education in practical politics.

By the fall of 1881, he had caught the attention of Joe Murray, one of the 21st District's leaders. Murray needed a candidate to run for the district's seat in the New York State legislature. Roosevelt agreed, and in November, he easily won election in the strongly Republican

Roosevelt married Alice Lee in 1880, when he was 22 and she was 19.

district. Some of Roosevelt's family and friends were embarrassed by his political success. They let him know that "politics were 'low'. . . and not controlled by gentlemen." As he pursued his political career, such snobbish opinions never bothered him or changed his course.

A Dude in the New York Assembly

Everyone noticed the stylishly dressed young man. He entered the chamber of the New York State Assembly carrying a gold-headed cane.

"Who's the dude?" Assemblyman John Walsh asked a colleague.

"That's Theodore Roosevelt of New York [City]."

Roosevelt's entrance as a new lawmaker was dramatic not only because of his clothes. At 23, he was the youngest member ever elected to the assembly. He continued to gain more than his share of attention and publicity, demonstrating the brave and sometimes reckless political temperament that would become his trademark. He quickly gained a reputation as an incorruptible but preachy *reformer.* He attacked political corruption wherever he found it, complaining most loudly about the secret alliances between wealthy businessmen who paid bribes to get their way and corrupt politicians and judges who took the bribes. "They are common thieves," he said of the businessmen. "They belong to that most dangerous of all classes, the wealthy criminal class."

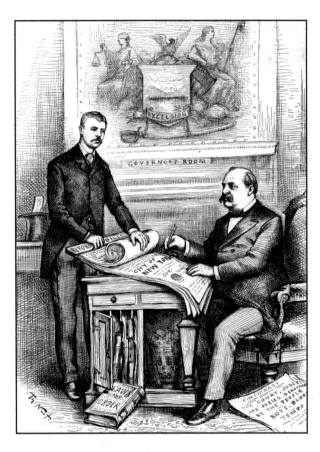

Young assemblyman Theodore Roosevelt discusses reform of New York City with Grover Cleveland, the governor of New York State. Cleveland was elected president in 1884 and again in 1892.

Roosevelt became a favorite of newspaper writers covering the assembly. They learned they could count on him for a good story and a colorful quote. Roosevelt saw the press as a great way to get his views directly to the people. The strategy often won public support for his positions and helped put pressure on his opponents. Roosevelt's alliance with the press would serve him well and cause his opponents deep frustration.

By the time he ran for reelection to the assembly in 1882, Roosevelt had dropped out of law school. He won reelection easily, and assembly Republicans elected him minority leader at the age of 24. "I rose like a rocket," he said later. In the fall of 1883, he was elected to a third one-year term.

Disaster

In February 1884 the Roosevelt rocket came crashing to earth.

On February 13, Theodore stared out the window of a train chugging slowly south from Albany to New York City. In his pocket were two telegrams. One announced the birth of his and Alice's daughter. The other announced that his mother was near death and his young wife dangerously ill.

Theodore was met at the door by his younger brother. "There is a curse on this house," Elliott said.

Early in the morning of February 14, Theodore's mother died. In another room, his wife Alice was near death. Her pregnancy had revealed a serious kidney ailment, and the delivery of her child had caused her kidneys to fail. Alice died that afternoon, Valentine's Day, cradled in her husband's arms. Theodore drew a thick, black X in his diary and wrote below it, "The light has gone out of my life."

On February 14, 1884, Roosevelt's mother and his young wife Alice died within a few hours in the same house. Roosevelt's diary expresses his feelings.

Dakota Ranchman

The deaths of his mother and wife were terrible blows. "He was a changed man," noted fellow assemblyman Isaac Hunt. "From that time on there was a sadness about his face that he never had before. It was a grief that he had in his soul."

That grief drove him to the western wilds of the Dakota Territory. During a visit in 1883, he had fallen in love with the open spaces of the frontier territory and bought a tract of ranch land. Now in 1884, as soon as the assembly adjourned in June, he retreated to the Dakotas to escape his heartache, leaving his infant daughter Alice in the care of his older sister. "Black care rarely sits behind a rider whose pace is fast enough," he wrote. He bought cattle, built a ranch house, and filled his days working and hunting.

Old cowhands snickered at the rich easterner dressed in fringed and beaded buckskin clothes and silver spurs. "I now look like a regular cowboy dandy," he admitted. In a land of tough cowboy curses, his strongest expression was "By Godfrey!" One day he sent his own ranch hands into fits of laughter when, instead of yelling "Get going!" he shouted, "Hasten forward quickly there!"

Still, Roosevelt's toughness was genuine. He earned the respect of the cowhands he employed by spending 18 hours a day in the saddle and tackling every job a cowhand must do—roping, branding, breaking horses, and riding

In the Dakota Territory, Roosevelt managed the Elk Horn Ranch (top) in present-day North Dakota. Today it is part of the Theodore Roosevelt National Park. Dakota cowhands laughed at Roosevelt's fancy western clothes (bottom), but they came to respect his boundless energy and willingness to work alongside them.

herd. He hunted bison and antelope, and traveled to Montana to shoot his first grizzly bear. One night in a saloon, he punched out a gun-toting bully who called him "Four Eyes" (making fun of his glasses) and demanded that Roosevelt buy drinks for everyone.

In his autobiography, Roosevelt wrote nostalgically about those Dakota days:

> We knew toil and hardship and hunger and thirst; and we saw men die
>
> violent deaths as they worked among the horses and cattle, or fought in
>
> evil feuds with one another, but we felt the beat of hardy life in our
>
> veins, and ours was the glory of work and the joy of living.

Roosevelt spent nearly three years in the Dakotas. He grew from a slender young man to a toughened outdoorsman. He also broadened his knowledge of a different America, far from the glitter of New York society and the refinement of Harvard, and he learned more about himself. "If it had not been for my years in North Dakota, I never would have become president of the United States," he said later.

By late 1886, though, something—and someone—was calling him to his true home.

Return to the Fray ———

During his Dakota years, Roosevelt made regular visits to New York. On one of them, in
1885, he happened to meet Edith Carow. The
two had been friends since childhood, but
now deeper feelings grew. Later that year,
they were engaged to be married, but Theodore asked Edith to keep the engagement a
secret for another year. During that time, a
widow or widower was expected to mourn for
at least two years before remarrying.

In the fall of 1886, Roosevelt's politi-
cal career came to life again. New York City
Republicans asked him to run for mayor in
November. Against two experienced candi-

Roosevelt married Edith Carow, a friend since childhood, in
December 1886.

dates, he had little chance to win, but Roosevelt threw all his energy into the campaign. "The Cowboy Candidate," as he was called, finished third, but the
campaign brought Roosevelt's name back to public notice. After the loss, he said,
"Well, anyway, I had a bully time."

Soon afterward, he and Edith sailed to England. They were married in London and enjoyed a European honeymoon. Intellectual and serious, Edith provided a steadying influence on her husband's excitable nature.

With a new wife and new political ambitions, Roosevelt knew his future lay in New York, not in the Dakotas. That winter confirmed his decision. A horrific winter storm nearly wiped out his cattle herd and damaged other investments in the territory. Altogether, he lost about $80,000—several million dollars in present-day money.

In 1887, the Roosevelts moved from New York City to a handsome 22-room mansion called Sagamore Hill, near Oyster Bay, New York. The new house stood on a hill near the shore of Long Island Sound, about 30 miles (48 km) from the city. In the years that followed, Sagamore Hill, with its woods, shore, and wildlife, often called Roosevelt and his growing family back to its comforts and warmth.

Washington, D.C.

In 1888, Roosevelt campaigned for Republican presidential candidate Benjamin Harrison. Harrison won a very close election, and when he took office in 1889, he appointed Roosevelt to the U.S. Civil Service Commission in Washington, D.C.

Civil service reform was a recent idea in 1889. *Civil servants* are those who are appointed to jobs in the government. For years, Democratic and Republican elected officials had rewarded thousands of friends and supporters by appointing them to these jobs. Some appointees were qualified, but many were not, and some collected their pay without even showing up for work. To correct these abuses, Congress had passed the Pendleton Civil Service Act in 1883. It required that many positions in the *federal government* (the national government) be given to applicants who proved qualified by passing civil service examinations.

The bill set up the Civil Service Commission to investigate cases in which the new act was not obeyed, but the commission had limited powers and a small budget. Many of the commissioners were reluctant to accuse powerful party leaders of breaking the law. As a young reformer, Theodore Roosevelt saw things differently. He was willing to investigate Democrats or Republicans who tried to get around these laws. He traveled the country investigating reports of shady dealings in awarding government jobs. He took special interest in the U.S. Post Office, then the largest government department, with jobs in every city and town. "I am a great believer in practical politics," he wrote Congressman Henry Cabot Lodge, "but when my duty is to enforce a law, that law is surely going to be enforced without fear or favor."

President Harrison was amused and irritated by Roosevelt's eagerness, commenting, "He wants to put an end to all the evil in the world between sunrise and sunset."

Roosevelt remained on the commission for six years and succeeded in bringing many abuses into public view. He was less successful in changing the behavior of party leaders, who continued to use federal jobs as rewards for party loyalty and service. Still, he learned much about the federal system, and he befriended many other young reformers who hoped to bring change as they gained more power in Washington.

Return to New York

By the spring of 1895, Roosevelt was ready for a change. A reform Republican mayor invited him to bring his reforming ways to the New York police department. Roosevelt was appointed one of four members of the Police Commission and was elected its president.

"New York's Finest," as the city's police force was called, was in terrible shape in the 1890s. Roosevelt later wrote:

From top to bottom the . . . police force was utterly demoralized. . . .

Venality and blackmail went hand-in-hand with the basest forms of low ward politics. . . . The policeman, the ward politician, the liquor seller, and the criminal alternately preyed on one another and helped one another prey on the general public.

Now Roosevelt had the chance to help clean up the mess.

The new commissioner knew he had to dramatize the problem. In the early hours of June 7, 1895, he met prize-winning reporter Jacob Riis to tour the streets in search of police officers on patrol. They found very few, since most had left their beats for a nap, a snack, or a beer. Finally, the investigators found two policemen chatting outside a liquor store. Standing in the shadows, Roosevelt asked, "Why don't you two men patrol your posts?" The officers seemed ready to threaten the disrespectful citizen, until he introduced himself as their boss. When they saw their mistake, they hurried back to their rounds.

"POLICEMEN DIDN'T DREAM THE PRESIDENT OF THE BOARD WAS CATCHING THEM NAPPING," read one headline the next day. Roosevelt went on other "midnight rambles," and soon lazy officers got the message. They were expected to do their jobs. The newspapers were effective at bringing issues to the public, and they also brought welcome publicity for Roosevelt himself.

Not all reforms were popular, however. New York's Sunday Excise Law made it illegal to sell alcoholic drinks on Sundays. For years, the law was rarely obeyed or enforced. In return for a bribe, police officers never reported a bar or saloon was open on Sunday. Roosevelt himself didn't agree with the law, but he believed it was the duty of the police to enforce all laws on the books. Under his direction, bar owners who opened on Sunday were closed down and slapped with heavy fines.

Many people admired Roosevelt's campaign for law and order. Yet many others were angry. Workers in poor neighborhoods, who prized a glass of beer or

Author, Author

Through much of his life, Theodore Roosevelt used his spare time to write books. He published his first book, *Summer Birds of the Adirondacks*, as a student at Harvard. Two years later, he published *The Naval War of 1812*. After returning from the Dakotas, he wrote *The Winning of the West* (1889), about the exploration and settlement of the western United States, which became widely popular.

Later, he wrote dozens of books, including biographies of U.S. leaders, accounts of his own travels and adventures, and his *Autobiography*. In addition, he published hundreds of magazine articles. While in the White House, he had little need to trust his speeches to a speechwriter. He could usually write them better himself.

Other presidents, including Thomas Jefferson, Woodrow Wilson, and John F. Kennedy, wrote and published important and popular books, but Theodore Roosevelt wrote more books on a wider range of subjects than any other president.

☆☆☆

wine on their only day off, heartily despised the police commissioner. Bar owners complained that enforcing the law cost them business they needed to survive. Corrupt politicians and police officers, who valued the bribes they had received on Sundays, complained as well. The political outcry was so great that the reform mayor did not seek reelection.

It seemed a good time for Roosevelt to take a new job. Fortunately, Republican William McKinley was elected president in 1896. When he took office, Roosevelt's friends—and his enemies—urged McKinley to appoint the troublesome reformer to a job in Washington. McKinley soon obliged, and Roosevelt resigned from the Police Commission. The *New York Times* paid tribute to Roosevelt's efforts to reform the police department, concluding, "The service he has rendered to the city is . . . in our judgment unequaled."

Chapter 3

War Fever

President McKinley received many recommendations for Theodore Roosevelt, but was reluctant to appoint him to the government. Roosevelt had a reputation for recklessness. "I want peace and I am told that your friend Theodore . . . is always getting into rows with everybody," McKinley told one Roosevelt friend. Finally, though, McKinley agreed to name the troublemaker assistant secretary of the navy.

A lover of ships and naval history since boyhood, Roosevelt dove eagerly into his new responsibilities. His boss, Secretary of the Navy John D. Long, was impressed by Roosevelt's grasp of the job. "I have right at hand a man possessed with more knowledge than I could acquire," Long said. Soon, he was taking long breaks from the office, leaving Roosevelt in charge. "The Secretary is away and I am having immense fun running the navy," Roosevelt told a friend.

Naval Power

It was an important moment to have responsibilities for the U.S. Navy. In the past 50 years, Great Britain had gained a worldwide empire, controlling huge areas and populations in Asia and Africa. France and Germany were not far behind. Britain's main weapons in this contest for new territories were its navy, second to none in the world, and its merchant fleet, which carried on trade in every corner of the globe.

Now Americans were asking what role the United States should play on the international stage. Leading merchants and traders feared that U.S. businesses might be shut out of world trade by the powerful colonial powers. Land speculators who had made fortunes in the American West were looking for new territories to buy and develop. Military leaders worried that the United States might someday be surrounded by the navies of powerful enemies. All of these groups urged the United States to get into the contest for overseas territories—and to strengthen its navy. Theodore Roosevelt agreed with them.

In 1895, a revolutionary band in Cuba began a war for independence from Spain, which had controlled the island for centuries. The Spanish government responded with brutal military force. U.S. newspapers sent reporters to Cuba and published lurid stories about the atrocities of the Spanish and the suffering of the Cuban patriots. They compared the war for Cuban independence to the American Revolution.

Roosevelt called on the United States to support the rebels' fight, preferably with U.S. ships and soldiers. "Better a thousand times err on the side of over-readiness to fight," he said in June 1897, "than to err on the side of tame submission to injury, or cold-blooded indifference to the misery of the oppressed."

President McKinley, who had fought bravely in the U.S. Civil War, was less eager for a fight, and he resisted going to war in Cuba. At one point he said, "I have been through one war, I have seen the dead piled up, and I do not want to see another."

A disaster in February 1898 made war all but unavoidable. The U.S. battleship *Maine* had been sent to Cuba to protect U.S. interests there. But on the night of February 15, a mysterious explosion ripped the ship apart, killing 265 U.S. seamen and officers. Within days, newspapers across the land were clamoring for a declaration of war. When a naval investigation concluded that a mine had been used to destroy the ship, the cries grew louder. "To Hell with Spain! Remember the *Maine!*" became a popular chant.

Anticipating war, Roosevelt had been working for months to prepare the navy if a war did begin. He ordered ships to load fuel and ammunition, and he positioned squadrons for an attack. Some of his orders worried Secretary Long, yet neither Long nor McKinley moved to block them.

The explosion of the U.S. battleship *Maine* in the harbor at Havana, Cuba, in February 1898 increased the eagerness of Americans to go to war against Spain. More than 250 U.S. Navy men were killed in the blast.

Finally, on April 21, the U.S. Congress declared war on Spain. Only nine days later, the U.S. Asiatic Squadron, commanded by Commodore George Dewey, attacked the Spanish fleet in the harbor at Manila, the capital of the Philippines, Spain's largest Asian possession. The Spanish fleet was destroyed.

Days later, Roosevelt resigned as assistant navy secretary. Now he wanted to taste the fighting for himself.

War Hero

"Father went to war last Thursday," wrote nine-year-old Kermit Roosevelt in a letter. By 1898, Theodore and Edith Roosevelt had five children of their own, plus Alice from Theodore's first marriage. Edith fell seriously ill that spring, but even that did not slow Roosevelt's personal rush to war. "I know now that I should have turned from my wife's deathbed to have answered the call," he later told a friend.

Why would a happy family man and promising public official risk everything to face bullets? Roosevelt believed that war offered the greatest measure of courage and manhood. He wanted to test himself, and he was afraid of appearing to be an armchair warrior. "For the last year I have preached war with Spain," he said. "I should feel distinctly ashamed . . . if I now failed to practice what I have preached." He may have remembered his embarrassment as a boy that his own father had not enlisted in the Civil War.

Roosevelt was commissioned a lieutenant colonel and helped organize the First U.S. Volunteer Cavalry Regiment. Some 23,000 applications poured in for the unique 1,000-man force. He helped choose frontiersmen who had special talents as horsemen and marksmen, then added top athletes from Ivy League colleges. The group was soon known as "Roosevelt's Rough Riders."

After weeks of training and delay, the U.S. invasion fleet arrived on the Cuban coast on June 22. Orders had reduced the Rough Riders to 560 fighters and

Fast Facts

THE SPANISH-AMERICAN WAR

Who: The U.S. against Spain.

Where: On land and sea in Cuba, Puerto Rico, and the Philippines

Why: The U.S. supported Cuban rebels fighting for their independence from Spain. U.S. expansionists saw the war as a chance to take control of Spanish territories.

When: Spain declared war on the U.S. April 20, 1898; fighting ended in July.

Outcome: The U.S. scored quick victories in Manila Harbor (May 1) and in Cuba (July 1–3); Spain asked for negotiations in August and the Treaty of Paris was signed December 10. It granted Cuba independence under U.S. protection; ceded Puerto Rico and Guam to the U.S.; and ceded the Philippines for a payment by the U.S. of $20 million.

forced them to leave nearly all of their horses in Florida. On foot, Roosevelt's "cavalry" joined the march into the island's steamy jungle east of the town of Santiago de Cuba.

On June 24, the Rough Riders saw their first action when Spanish snipers opened fire. "We were caught in a clear case of ambush . . . the hottest, nastiest fight I ever imagined," wrote war correspondent Richard Harding Davis. When in trouble—in politics or war—Roosevelt's instinct was to attack. That's what he did now, ordering his men to charge. This drove the snipers off, but not before 8 of his men were killed and 34 were wounded.

A week later, on July 1, Roosevelt led his men in the charge up Kettle Hill on the San Juan Heights. That same day the fort in Santiago surrendered. Two days later, the Spanish fleet was destroyed by an American naval force while trying to escape from Santiago harbor. The war in Cuba effectively ended after eleven days of fighting. Roosevelt became the most celebrated hero of the war. From that time forward, he preferred the title of "colonel" to any other.

An artist's conception of Roosevelt leading the charge up Kettle Hill. In reality, Roosevelt and his men were on foot, but illustrations like this one helped make Roosevelt a national hero.

Hawaii

As the Spanish-American War was coming to a climax, President McKinley gained control of another offshore possession for the United States. Five years earlier, a group of American sugar planters (with the help of U.S. Marines) had forced out Hawaii's native Queen Liliuokalani. The planters established their own government and requested that the United States *annex* the islands, making them part of the United States.

President Cleveland, who took office in 1893, opposed annexation, but was not able to remove the new government. When McKinley took office in 1897, he favored annexation. He argued that its naval base would be useful to the United States and raised fears that Japan or Germany might claim the base instead. He finally persuaded Congress to approve the annexation of Hawaii on July 7, 1898, days after the decisive U.S. victories over Spain in Cuba.

Hawaii became an official territory of the United States in 1900 and became the 50th state in 1959.

☆ ☆ ☆

The Boy Governor

In August 1898, Colonel Theodore Roosevelt returned from Cuba the most famous man in the United States. Popularity meant easy votes, and Republican leaders asked him to run for governor of New York, then the country's most populous state. Roosevelt agreed.

Roosevelt campaigned across the state. He punched his right hand into his palm while his even teeth clacked together, as if biting off words in chunks. He described his idea of leadership with an African proverb that would become his most famous slogan: "Speak softly and carry a big stick; you will go far." In other words, "Don't brag and bluster, but be ready to back up your words with action."

The campaign made use of Roosevelt's war exploits, and even used Rough Riders as campaign speakers. Sometimes the results were amusing. "He was there in the midst of us," ex-sergeant Buck Taylor told voters, "and when it came to the great day he led us up San Juan Hill like sheep to the slaughter and so he will lead you."

Running as a reformer as well as war hero, Roosevelt won the November election by a narrow margin. Just 40 years old, the "boy governor" charged into controversy in the state capital. He pushed for laws limiting the long working hours of women and children. He sought better conditions for workers in factories aptly called sweatshops. He even signed a law imposing a tax on corporations. Business leaders, nearly all important Republicans, complained bitterly to the state Republican boss, Senator Thomas Platt.

Platt was used to commanding all Republicans in New York, but Roosevelt was unwilling to take orders. By 1900, Platt's patience with Roosevelt was exhausted. "I don't want him raising hell in my state any longer," Platt said. Roosevelt was up for reelection. How could Platt get rid of a popular governor without angering Roosevelt supporters?

The wily boss found the perfect solution. President McKinley was running for reelection that fall, and he needed a vice presidential candidate. Platt began a campaign to get the nomination for Governor Roosevelt. If the campaign succeeded, Roosevelt would land in a place of honor, but far from New York politics.

Mark Hanna, President McKinley's closest political adviser, was horrified at the thought of Roosevelt as vice president. "Don't any of you realize that there's only one life between this madman and the White House?" he com-

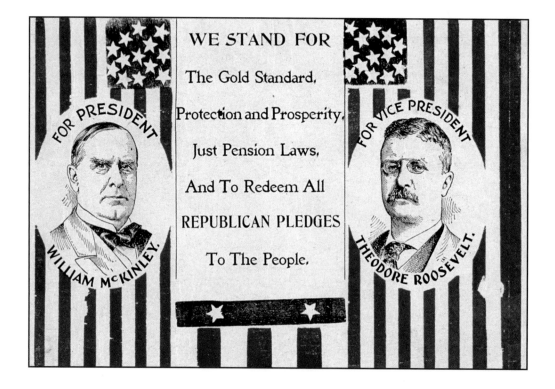

WE STAND FOR
The Gold Standard,
Protection and Prosperity,
Just Pension Laws,
And To Redeem All
REPUBLICAN PLEDGES
To The People.

FOR PRESIDENT
WILLIAM McKINLEY.

FOR VICE PRESIDENT
THEODORE ROOSEVELT.

In 1900, Roosevelt's popularity helped him gain the Republican nomination for vice president. He was the running mate of President William McKinley.

plained. Roosevelt was not very interested in any case. "The vice presidency is not an office in which I could *do* anything," he told a friend.

At the Republican Convention that summer, Roosevelt's popularity with the delegates overcame Hanna's objections and his own. Roosevelt himself appeared on the floor wearing his Rough Rider army hat. An observer clearly understood its meaning. "Gentlemen, that's an acceptance hat," he said. On the first ballot, the convention voted 925 to 1 to nominate Roosevelt for vice president. The only "no" vote was cast by Roosevelt himself.

In November, McKinley and Roosevelt easily defeated the Democratic ticket led by William Jennings Bryan. One Republican campaign worker said, "I feel sorry for McKinley. He has a man of destiny behind him."

Chapter **4**

September 1901 —————————————————

On September 6, 1901, President McKinley was greeting visitors to a Pan-American Exposition in Buffalo, New York. A young man stepped up to shake the president's hand. The man's right hand appeared bandaged with a handkerchief, but it really concealed a pistol. The man, Leon Czolgosz, fired two shots. McKinley fell, seriously wounded. Czolgosz was an *anarchist*, who believed in abolishing all governments.

Vice president Roosevelt hurried to McKinley's bedside. After three days, it appeared the president was recovering. "The President is coming along splendidly," Roosevelt wrote to his sister. The president's aides sent Roosevelt away, hoping this would reassure worried Americans.

Roosevelt traveled with his wife and friends to New York's Adirondack Mountains on a hiking trip. On September 13, the group

On September 5, 1901, President McKinley appears at the Pan-American Exposition in Buffalo, New York. The next day, while shaking hands at a reception there, McKinley was shot and mortally wounded.

was returning from climbing Mount Marcy, New York's highest peak, when a ranger came hurrying up the trail with a telegram. "I instinctively knew he had bad news," Roosevelt later recalled, "—the worst news in the world." President McKinley was near death. Roosevelt hurried down the mountain to the nearest railroad station. There another telegram reported that the president had died.

After traveling all night, Roosevelt reached Buffalo on September 14. There he reassured McKinley's grieving advisers, saying, "It shall be my aim to continue, absolutely unbroken, the policy of President McKinley for the peace, the prosperity, and the honor of our country." He took the oath of office at the home of a friend. Now Theodore Roosevelt was the 26th president of the United States. At 42, he was the youngest chief executive in the nation's history.

Mark Hanna was not the only Republican worried about the new president's pro-reform record and combative nature. Roosevelt realized that he must act cautiously at first to soothe a shocked public and government. He met with political leaders and promised stability. He asked the members of McKinley's *cabinet* (main advisers) to stay on, again to signal steadiness.

In truth, Theodore Roosevelt was more conservative than he seemed. He was above all a believer in "practical politics," always calculating what goals were achievable as well as desirable. He summarized the problem later in a letter to his son Kermit: "I pass my days in a state of exasperation, first with the fools who do

Roosevelt brought a new attitude to the presidency. While other presidents seemed weighed down by the responsibilities of the office, Roosevelt seemed to enjoy every minute of his time in power.

not want to do any of the things that ought to be done, and second, with the equally obnoxious fools who insist upon so much that they cannot get anything."

Roosevelt sent his first annual message to Congress in December. In it he lamented the "great calamity" of President McKinley's assassination. Then he provided a carefully worded outline of his administration's plans. The message stirred little controversy, causing the New York *Post* to comment: "The 'Rough Rider,' . . . the impetuous youth of a year ago, has disappeared."

Those who knew Roosevelt well knew that he was just biding his time. He enjoyed wielding power, and he would prove to be very good at it. In the coming years, Roosevelt would put the *executive branch* (the presidency and its departments) at the heart of national politics.

Square Dealing

Big business was the first major target of Roosevelt's reform program. Business owners were forming *trusts*, groups of companies in the same industry governed by the same directors. Trusts used their power to drive competing companies out of business and take control of the industry. In his first message to Congress Roosevelt said, "There is a widespread conviction in the minds of the American people that the great corporations known as trusts are in certain of their features and tendencies hurtful to the general welfare."

Roosevelt and Race

In 1901, 36 years after the end of slavery, African Americans were suffering through a period of harsh discrimination and deadly terror at the hands of white racists. The treatment of African Americans was a painful issue that had vexed earlier presidents. Roosevelt soon learned why.

On October 16, 1901, black leader Booker T. Washington came to dinner at the White House to discuss the political situation in the South. Dr. Washington was the founder and head of the Tuskegee Institute, an Alabama college for African Americans. He was the first African American man ever invited to dine with a U.S. president.

African Americans happily greeted the White House dinner as a sign that the new president might take their suffering seriously. On the other hand, many southern whites were furious. The Memphis *Scimitar* called the president's willingness to eat with a black man "the most damnable outrage ever perpetrated by any citizen of the United States."

Publicly, Roosevelt stated he would have Washington "to dine just as often as I please." Privately, though, he knew he must not go too far in offending white southerners. Dr. Washington and other African Americans would return to the Roosevelt White House for meetings, but were never again honored with a presidential dinner.

☆ ☆ ☆

Roosevelt believed the federal government was the only watchdog big enough and strong enough to stand up to the trusts. As companies grew larger and eliminated competition, they could charge whatever they wished for their

EQUALITY

Roosevelt's controversial White House dinner with African American Booker T. Washington was portrayed by one magazine with a surprising tablecloth, spelling out the significance of the event.

product or service, and they could pay overworked laborers as little as they wished.

In February 1902, Roosevelt announced his trust-busting test case. J. P. Morgan, the most powerful financier of his time, had announced plans to combine three railroads that served the Northwest into a single unit, the Northern Securities Company. Roosevelt asked Attorney General Philander Knox to bring suit against the merger of the railroads, challenging it under the Sherman

Antitrust Act of 1890. In 1904, the Supreme Court decided in the government's favor, and Northern Securities was broken up.

Roosevelt emphasized that he wasn't against all big businesses or trusts, just those that used their power to abuse workers and overcharge customers. His administration brought court cases against other trusts in the beef, oil, and tobacco industries. The courts ruled to break up these companies or fine them. The government's success signaled U.S. businesses that they had a responsibility not just to their own profits but also to the American public. That message was reinforced when Congress established the Department of Commerce and Labor in 1903. This government agency helped give consumers and workers a voice in Washington, where leading businessmen were already well represented.

In 1902, Roosevelt took action in a major dispute between business and labor. In May, 150,000 members of the United Mine Workers union (UMW) went on *strike* against Pennsylvania anthracite coal mines, walking off their jobs to protest low pay and unsafe conditions. The mine owners and operators hired non-union replacement workers and refused to *negotiate* (discuss union grievances). Striking miners began destroying property and terrorizing the replacement workers.

As summer turned to autumn, the crisis grew. In 1902, the U.S. economy ran mainly on coal, which was used to make steel, to generate electricity, and to power railroad locomotives. Most important, it was used to heat most homes and

This group photograph of Pennsylvania coal miners suggests the demanding nature of their jobs. The coal dust which smeared everything also caused serious lung ailments.

public buildings. That fall, schools began to close for lack of heat, and desperate people seized railcars filled with coal to carry off fuel for their stoves. Coal prices quadrupled. If there was no coal during the winter, Roosevelt predicted "the most terrible riots that this country has ever seen."

Conflict between large companies and their workers was one of the most explosive issues of the time. Although earlier presidents had expressed sympathy for workers and unions, the government almost always backed the corporation, even supplying soldiers to force a strike's end.

Roosevelt tried a new approach. In October, he invited both sides to a meeting in Washington. Even though he had no legal right to interfere, he viewed himself as the representative of the American people, who had a huge stake in the outcome. He urged both sides to submit their dispute to *arbitration* (negotiation before a group of arbitrators who can determine a final settlement). The union representatives were willing to accept the plan, but mine operators rejected it.

Having tried to "speak softly" through negotiation, Roosevelt was ready with a "big stick." He quietly ordered U.S. troops to prepare to take over the mines. At the same time, Roosevelt's secretary of war, Elihu Root, was in intense discussions with J. P. Morgan, who had stepped in to represent the mine operators. With time running out, both sides agreed to arbitration. They agreed that the workers should go back to work while a seven-member arbitration panel heard arguments from both sides and reached a fair settlement.

The agreement ended the crisis, and within weeks coal was being shipped again from the mines. The arbitration panel later required the companies to increase wages by 10 percent, to reduce the workday, and to take measures to

A cartoonist suggests that Roosevelt's success in forcing major coal companies to submit strike issues to arbitration was one of his most important accomplishments.

improve workers' safety. It also recommended that operators raise coal prices by 10 percent, which they promptly did.

Afterward, Roosevelt outlined a new philosophy of government involvement in business and labor disputes: "The labor unions shall have a square deal, and the corporations shall have a square deal, and in addition all private citizens shall have a square deal." The term "Square Deal" came to represent Roosevelt's willingness to use the power of the presidency and the federal government to

The Teddy Bear

DRAWING
THE LINE
IN MISSISSIPPI

This cartoon showing Roosevelt refusing to shoot at a small captive bear appeared just as stuffed bears were being introduced in toy stores. The popular stuffed toys soon were known as teddy bears.

In November 1902, Roosevelt traveled to Mississippi to hunt bear. Game was scarce, however, and the president did not get off a shot. Finally, a guide cornered a small black bear, tied it up, and crippled it so that the president could have a chance to shoot it. Roosevelt arrived to find an injured, helpless creature. He refused to take a shot and walked away in disgust. Someone else put the bear out of its misery.

The incident caught the public's imagination. They approved of his refusal to shoot a helpless animal. A cartoon of "Teddy" and the bear appeared in the Washington *Post*. (In truth, Roosevelt hated the nickname "Teddy.") By chance, stuffed toy bears began appearing in toy stores about the same time. The bears soon became linked with the president, and ever since, small children have been cuddling up with their teddy bears.

promote fair play throughout the U.S. economy. His actions in the coal strike raised his popularity to a new high.

Panama

NEW REPUBLIC MAY ARISE TO GRANT CANAL

The State of Panama Ready to Secede if the

Treaty is Rejected by the Colombian Congress

ROOSEVELT IS SAID TO ENCOURAGE THE IDEA

This headline in the New York *World* in June 1903 summarized one of the president's most daring and controversial moves. Pressure had been building for years to build a canal across Central America to make it possible for ships to pass from the Atlantic to the Pacific Oceans without traveling thousands of miles around the tip of South America.

By 1903, U.S. engineers had concluded that the best route for a canal was across Panama, the northernmost province of the country of Colombia. Roosevelt was determined to negotiate rights to a narrow strip of land so that construction of the canal could begin. There was only one problem. The Colombian government rejected the terms of a *treaty* (agreement) offered by the United States. It wanted more money and more limits on U.S. authority. Negotiations dragged on for months. "The Colombian people proved absolutely impossible to deal with," Roosevelt complained. "They are not merely corrupt. They are governmentally utterly corrupt."

Fortunately for the president, there was a group in Panama that wanted to break away from Colombia and form an independent nation. In Roosevelt's mind, this offered an opening. If the Panamanians wanted independence, the United States stood ready to help. U.S. representatives encouraged the independence movement, and Roosevelt sent a warship to stand offshore in support of Panama. The Panamanians drove the Colombian government from their province in November 1903 and set up a new government that was recognized by the United States. Only weeks later, Panama ratified a treaty giving the United States perpetual possession of the Canal Zone, a strip of land 10 miles (16 km) wide from the Atlantic to the Pacific. After more than ten years of construction, the Panama Canal opened for business in 1914.

Roosevelt's behind-the-scenes scheming to secure a canal route proved controversial. "This mad plunge of ours [into Panama] is simply and solely a vulgar and mercenary venture, without rag to cover its . . . shame," wrote the New York *Post*. Even Roosevelt's cabinet members questioned the justice of his actions, but Roosevelt never doubted the rightness of what he'd done. He viewed the canal as being "in the vital interests of civilization."

Roosevelt acted aggressively to gain land for building the Panama Canal across nearly 50 miles (80 km) of tropical jungle. It was the largest and most costly engineering project in the world up to that time.

Hitting His Stride ─────────────────────

By 1904, Roosevelt had hit his stride as president. Like a star athlete, he performed best under pressure, reveling in the challenges and powers of office. The White House overflowed with his vitality. In a time before movie stars, Roosevelt was the nation's leading celebrity. The public delighted in news of the president's antics, whether he was jumping his horse over fences, throwing foreign ministers to the floor in judo demonstrations, or leading finely dressed diplomats on an "obstacle walk"—a fast-paced hike in a straight line crawling under or over whatever stood in the way.

The White House Gang

Roosevelt's family proved a big political asset. The energy and mischief of his children became popular news, and helped personalize the presidency. The Roosevelt kids together with their cousins and friends were called "the White House Gang." The two youngest boys, Archie and Quentin, sledded down the main staircase on metal trays. They plastered fusty presidential portraits with spitballs. The broad hallways echoed with clacks, rumbles, and thumps of roller skates and stilts. Quentin once sneaked the family pony to the second floor to cheer up Archie as he lay sick in bed. The president joined in whenever he could, sometimes leading a game of "bear" where he roared and chased the kids around. "You must

always remember that the president is about six," one friend warned a group of diplomats.

Then there was Alice. By 1904, she had grown into a lovely, saucy 20-year-old who loved to shock people. "If you haven't got anything nice to say about anybody, come sit next to me," she once told a dinner companion. When she went out, she often managed to "lose" the Secret Service agents assigned to her. Once a friend asked Roosevelt why he couldn't control his eldest daughter. Eyes twinkling, he replied, "I can be president or I can attend to Alice. I can't do both."

☆☆☆

Roosevelt and his family about the time he became president. From left to right, they are Quentin, father Theodore, Theodore Jr., Archie, Alice (Roosevelt's daughter by his first wife), Kermit, mother Edith, and Ethel.

As the 1904 presidential election approached, it became clear that Roosevelt would cease being the "accidental president" and be elected in his own right. "As far as I can see there is no need of an election," commented one editorial writer. Roosevelt's record and larger-than-life personality swamped the Democratic candidate, Alton B. Parker. He won 7.6 million popular votes to Parker's

Vice President Charles W. Fairbanks

At the 1904 Republican Convention Charles W. Fairbanks (1852–1918) was nominated for vice president to help win Indiana and reassure Republican business leaders. A tall man with a cold personality, the Indiana senator was one of the Republicans' "Old Guard." One writer dubbed the Roosevelt-Fairbanks ticket "the Hot Tamale and the Indiana Icicle."

Fairbanks made a fortune as a railroad lawyer. By the 1880s, he dominated Indiana's Republican party and in 1896 was elected to the U.S. Senate, where he served as a spokesman and supporter of President McKinley. McKinley sent Senator Fairbanks on a fact-finding mission to Alaska, where he took a strong interest in settling a dispute on the Alaska-Canada boundary. In 1903, on the recommendation of pioneering Alaska judge James Wickersham, a new inland gold-rush town was named Fairbanks in his honor.

Fairbanks played little part in the second Roosevelt administration. He hoped to win the Republican presidential nomination in 1908, but Roosevelt supported Secretary of War William Howard Taft instead.

★ ★ ☆

5.1 million and gained 336 electoral votes to Parker's 140. Roosevelt couldn't help but marvel at the results: "I have the greatest popular majority and the greatest electoral majority ever given a candidate for President."

Then, on election night, Roosevelt shocked his supporters. He declared he would not run again in 1908. He would come to regret that promise.

Chapter 5

Peacemaker

On March 4, 1905, a cold, blustery day, Theodore Roosevelt took the oath of office on the steps of the Capitol. In a brief inaugural speech he proclaimed, "Toward all other nations, large and small, our attitude must be one of cordial and sincere friendship." He soon backed up these words with action.

Russia and Japan had been at war over control of Korea and part of China for more than a year. The Japanese army and navy were thrashing the Russians, but neither side would call for negotiations. A week after his inauguration, Roosevelt let both countries know that he was willing to help negotiate a peace settlement. At first, there was no response.

Then on May 27, the Japanese navy destroyed the Russian fleet at the battle of Tsushima. Russia was defeated, but Japanese

At Roosevelt's inauguration in 1905, many privileged spectators got to stand along the roof of the Capitol. The president took the oath of office at the stand in the middle of the picture.

forces and resources were exhausted as well. In early June, the two countries requested that Roosevelt oversee peace talks. Diplomats from the two proud countries met in Portsmouth, New Hampshire, that August, but negotiations soon bogged down. The Japanese wanted Russia to pay indemnities, money to make up for the losses Japan had suffered. Russia refused to consider such payments, and demanded the return of Sakhalin, a large island the Japanese had captured. The negotiators' stubborn behavior exasperated Roosevelt. "The Japanese ask too much, but the Russians are ten times worse," he wrote.

He went to work behind the scenes, encouraging and badgering the diplomats to shift their positions. He told the Russians bluntly that they faced political and military disaster if the war continued. He told the Japanese that another year of fighting would cost more money than Russia could pay in reparations. Finally his arguments carried the day. The Japanese gave up the demand for payments and Russia agreed to divide Sakhalin. After the treaty was signed, Roosevelt privately remarked, "It's a mighty good thing for Russia and a mighty good thing for Japan . . . [and] a mighty good thing for *me,* too!" The following year he won the famed Nobel Peace Prize for his role in ending the Russo-Japanese War.

Consumer Legislation

In 1906 Roosevelt continued his crusade for more consumer protections and fairer business practices in the United States. Many abuses were being uncovered by young investigative reporters, who were writing articles and books exposing corruption and wrongdoing. Roosevelt responded to their stories, but sometimes grew weary of their sensational reporting. With a mixture of amusement and criticism, he nicknamed them "muckrakers," for the workers who cleaned out horses' stables each day.

One famous example of muckraking was *The Jungle*, a book by Upton Sinclair which painted a sickening picture of the meatpacking industry. The meatpackers observed no sanitation laws, often sold tainted or rotten meat, and were endangering the health of consumers and workers alike. In response, Congress passed the Pure Food and Drug Act in June 1906, and Roosevelt signed it into law.

That year also saw the passage of the Hepburn Act, which gave the federal government more muscle to regulate the railroads. It included powers to prevent the railroads from charging "unjust or unreasonable rates," as well as authority to rein in unfair and unsafe practices.

The Jungle by Upton Sinclair told the sickening story of the meatpacking industry, which observed few rules of cleanliness and often sold the meat of diseased animals. The book helped bring the passage of federal laws requiring meat inspection.

Conservation

Roosevelt's efforts to turn the federal government into a giant watchdog did not please all Americans. Since the days of the American Revolution, many citizens had a strong distrust of overbearing central government. Now Roosevelt's proposals, one newspaper complained, represented "the most amazing program of centralization that any President of the United States has ever recommended."

In 1907, Roosevelt's reform legislation was slowed by increasing opposition. Because he had promised not to run for reelection in 1908, opponents in Congress believed they could stall new proposals until after the election, hoping for a less active and reformist president. The stalling irritated the president, but he found a new way to turn his ideas into policy.

One of the president's pet causes was the preservation of wilderness lands and conservation of natural resources. He learned that he could take many steps to advance these goals without the approval of Congress. Using executive orders, he blocked misuse of forests, important wildlife areas, vital waterways, and natural wonders such as the Grand Canyon. He assembled a conference of state and territorial governors to discuss conservation. "As a people we have the right and duty . . . to protect ourselves and our children against the wasteful development of our natural resources," he told them. He saw the preservation of these resources,

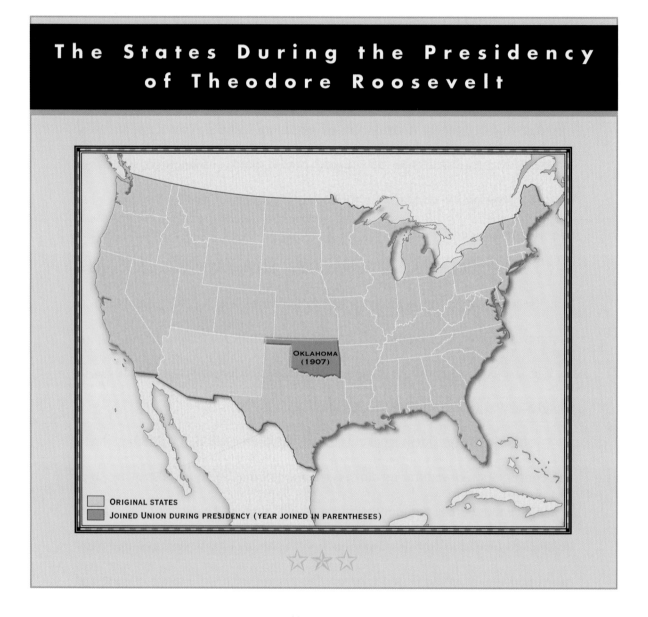

OKLAHOMA
(1907)

ORIGINAL STATES
JOINED UNION DURING PRESIDENCY (YEAR JOINED IN PARENTHESES)

not just as sources of inspiration and beauty, but as important stores of natural products for later use.

The Great White Fleet

An international dispute helped end his presidency in truly Rooseveltian style. Thousands of Japanese immigrants had moved to California, where they proved to be industrious and intelligent workers. Other Californians came to resent the success of the Japanese, however, and the state had passed laws to *discriminate against* Japanese citizens, restricting where they could work and where their children could go to school. The government of Japan grew agitated over tales of California's abuse of Japanese families. Recently successful in their war against Russia, the Japanese even hinted at war.

Roosevelt was disturbed by California's bigotry and tried to use his influence to temper the state's worst abuses. "Our people act infamously when they wrong in any way the Japanese who are here," he said. Still, he felt he must respond to Japan's veiled threats against the United States.

In December 1907, Roosevelt personally saw off 16 battleships from Hampton Roads, Virginia. This "Great White Fleet" was the greatest display of naval power ever brought together in one squadron. Its mission was to make a goodwill cruise around the world, and it received invitations from many countries

The Great White Fleet returns to U.S. waters in 1909 after its goodwill trip around the world. Roosevelt was there to greet it weeks before he left the presidency.

on its route, including Japan. The ships made a strong impression, and Roosevelt's underlying message was clear: the United States was now a world power and every world port was within reach of its navy.

First Lady Edith Roosevelt

Edith Kermit Carow Roosevelt (1861–1948) served as first lady in the lively Roosevelt White House. She had devoted much of her energy to raising six children, five of them her own, and Alice, Theodore Roosevelt's daughter by his first wife. Yet she was an avid reader and shared a love of the outdoors with her husband.

As first lady, Edith displayed her talents as a hostess and homemaker. Theodore gave her the nickname "Spotless Edie" for her love of tidiness. She oversaw the greatest restoration in White House history and helped bring the role of first lady out of the shadows and into the public eye.

Edith Carow Roosevelt provided quiet support for her husband in the White House and devoted much of her time to raising their growing family.

Edith Roosevelt did not take a public role in political discussion, but like many presidential wives, she served as an unofficial adviser to her husband. Theodore's niece Eleanor (who would someday be first lady herself) later wrote, "[Theodore] may have made his own decisions, but talking with [Edith] seemed to clarify things for him."

☆ ☆ ☆

Fourteen months later, in February 1909, the fleet returned and Roosevelt was there to welcome them back. By that time, less than a month remained in his term. "I could not ask a finer concluding scene to my administration," he said as the massive warships rumbled into port.

A New President

Roosevelt knew he would sorely miss the power of the presidency. He believed the best thing he could do was pick a successor who would carry on the work of reform that he had begun. Long before the 1908 election he settled on William Howard Taft, who served in his cabinet as secretary of war. The two men were close friends, and Roosevelt was confident of Taft's abilities. "If we can elect [Taft] President, we achieve all that could be achieved by continuing me in office," he said.

Taft was easily nominated at the Republican Convention and defeated Democrat William Jennings Bryan (who was running for the third time) by more than a million votes.

Roosevelt had already decided to make a long trip to Africa to hunt big game as soon as he left office. His main reason, he told a friend, was to be sure that no one could "do Taft the injustice of accusing him of permitting me to run the job."

Roosevelt with his handpicked successor, William Howard Taft, who was elected president in 1908. In 1912 Roosevelt ran against Taft, and both men lost to Democrat Woodrow Wilson.

For 10 months, Theodore and son Kermit, 19, hunted big game in East Africa as part of a large expedition. They killed 11 elephants, 17 lions, 20 rhinoceroses, and hundreds of smaller creatures, most of them later displayed in museums. Roosevelt also wrote several books and articles describing his adventures.

On his way home, Roosevelt toured Europe, where he was hailed with great fanfare. When he arrived in New York in June 1910, he received another stirring welcome and a ticker-tape parade from his fellow New Yorkers. "Such a

Ever adventurous, Roosevelt rode a camel in the Sudan during his world tour after leaving the White House.

shout went up from the shore as to waken the stones," reported an eyewitness. Roosevelt's popularity seemed only to have grown while he was gone.

The retired president did not like what Taft was doing as president, however. In his view, the new administration was undoing many of the reforms Roosevelt had championed. One particular sore point was that Taft had dismissed the men who had worked hardest with Roosevelt on conservation programs. Reform Republicans urged Roosevelt to challenge Taft, perhaps even to run once again for president in 1912. Roosevelt, still in his early 50s, was still full of energy and ambition. At first he dismissed the idea, but he was tempted by it.

Roosevelt's refusal to support his successor helped create a serious split in the Republican party. Most conservative leaders, including many businessmen, gravitated toward Taft, while progressive Republicans wanted Roosevelt to make a comeback. "Roosevelt for President" clubs began springing up across the country. In February 1912, Roosevelt made his decision. "My hat is in the ring!" Roosevelt shouted to a reporter who asked if he was going to run. "The fight is on and I am stripped to the buff."

Since leaving office, Roosevelt had grown more progressive. Now he favored even more government activism to protect worker and consumer rights. He wanted to end child labor and give women the right to vote. He attacked the courts for ruling in favor of big corporations, calling for presidential power to overrule such decisions. Critics called him a "madman" and warned he would lead the country to economic and social ruin.

For the first time, primary elections allowed ordinary Republicans to help nominate a presidential candidate. Roosevelt and Taft ran against each other in ten states, and Roosevelt won in nine of them. Taft had control of the National Convention, however. His supporters rounded up delegates from non-primary states to make sure that Taft received the nomination.

Roosevelt's furious supporters marched out of the convention hall. "If you wish me to make a fight, I will make it!" Roosevelt told them that night. With his blessing, they established the Progressive party and nominated Roosevelt as its presidential candidate. When a reporter asked about Roosevelt's health, he had a typically colorful answer. "I'm as strong as a bull

THE LATEST ARRIVAL AT THE POLITICAL ZOO

In 1912, Roosevelt ran for president on the ticket of the Progressive or Bull Moose party. This cartoon shows the new political animal, which wears Rooseveltian spectacles and flashes a Rooseveltian smile.

moose!" he said, pounding his chest. Instantly, the Progressive party became known as the Bull Moose party.

The campaign was a nasty affair, and it nearly ended in tragedy. Taft and Roosevelt, longtime friends, had not spoken for months, and now they were fierce opponents, exchanging accusations and insults. Others were angry, too. When Roosevelt came to Milwaukee, a gunman stepped from the crowd and shot him in his broad chest. The bullet passed through his coat, 50 folded pages of his speech, and a case for his glasses before lodging below his ribs. In his blood-soaked shirt, the Bull Moose still delivered a speech before going to the hospital. Luckily, he was not badly hurt.

Roosevelt failed to win the election, fighting another Republican on one hand and Woodrow Wilson, a Democrat almost as progressive as he was, on the other. Wilson was elected with more than a million votes more than Roosevelt. President Taft finished a humiliating third, winning only two states.

"We have fought the good fight, we have kept the faith, and we have nothing to regret," Roosevelt wrote afterward. Other Republicans disagreed.

The "Great Adventure"

That 1912 election proved Theodore Roosevelt's last great electoral battle. He retired to Sagamore Hill, where he wrote his autobiography and other books and

The Progressives

Roosevelt's reform agenda as president had been part of the progressive movement, which affected both parties. In general, it sought to make government more responsive to average Americans. It presented itself as an alternative to big-money politics and shady party "machines," organizations that controlled politics in many big cities and some states.

Planks in the progressives' platform included more antitrust laws, guaranteeing women the vote, an income tax, the creation of the Federal Reserve System to better manage the nation's currency, and the direct election of senators. (Following the Constitution, U.S. senators were still elected by state legislatures, not directly by voters.)

After Roosevelt's defeat in 1912, many progressives found a home in the Democratic party. They rallied around President Woodrow Wilson, a reform Democrat, and helped accomplish many of the movement's goals during his years in office. The Progressive party lost its leader in 1916, when Roosevelt returned to the Republican party and supported its candidates.

☆ ☆ ☆

articles. He could not stay still for long, however. In early 1914, he traveled in South America with his son Kermit. They joined an expedition to explore the dense jungles of Brazil and map the River of Doubt. The ex-president nearly lost his life in an accident, but survived to see the Brazilian government rename the river Rio Roosevelt in his honor.

That same year, a disastrous war broke out in Europe. Roosevelt immediately called for the United States to join the fight alongside Great Britain and France against Germany and Austria. Instead, President Wilson carefully maintained U.S. neutrality, much to the aging Rough Rider's frustration. Wilson succeeded in keeping the country out of the war and was reelected in 1916. The war continued, however, drawing the U.S. government ever closer to joining the battle.

Sagamore Hill, the Roosevelt home near Oyster Bay, New York, to which the former president and his wife retired. Today it is a national historic site.

Fast Facts

WORLD WAR I

Who: The Allies (Great Britain, France, Italy, Russia, the U.S., and others) against the Central Powers (Germany, Austria, the Ottoman Empire, and others)

Where: In Europe and western Asia and at sea

When: Began August 1914; the U.S. declared war in April 1917. Ended November 11, 1918, after the German government requested an armistice.

Why: Simmering disputes over territory combined with overlapping alliances dragged all of Europe into war. Officially neutral, the U.S. still found ways to support the Allies. This caused Germany to declare submarine warfare on American shipping in early 1917. This triggered the U.S. declaration of war.

Outcome: The Versailles Treaty, signed June 28, 1919, reduced the territories of the losing nations and set up many new nations, including Czechoslovakia, Poland, and Yugoslavia. Signers agreed to form the League of Nations to help resolve future disputes. The U.S. Senate refused to approve the treaty or join the League.

Early in 1917, Germany declared total submarine warfare against U.S. ships for their role in supplying the Allies. In April, Wilson asked Congress for a declaration of war. Roosevelt immediately asked to form a volunteer force similar to the Rough Riders, but the Wilson administration refused. Roosevelt was nearly 60, too old to lead another charge, but his four sons enlisted. As one of them said, "It's rather up to us to practice what Father preaches." Ted and Archie served as officers in the U.S. Army, while Kermit became a captain in the British forces. Quentin trained as a pilot in the fledgling U.S. air service.

In 1918, the arrival of fresh U.S. troops helped turn the tide against Germany, and in November, German leaders sued for an armistice. The guns fell silent and peace negotiations began.

Before the armistice, Roosevelt suffered the worst loss any father can bear. In July, Quentin, his youngest son, had flown into his first combat. Before the month was out, news arrived that the 20-year-old had been shot down and killed. In a tribute to "Q" Roosevelt wrote, "Only those are fit to live who do not fear to die; and none are fit to die who have shrunk from the joy of life and the duty of life. Both life and death are part of the same Great Adventure."

Theodore Roosevelt in 1918 with his granddaughter. Already in failing health, he died the following year.

In private, though, he was not so brave. "There is no use of my writing about Quentin," he wrote, "for I should break down if I tried."

Now the ex-president faced the second part of his own Great Adventure. His health had been failing, and Quentin's death was a terrible emotional blow that he never got over. He continued to write and publish, but his fire was going out. On January 6, 1919, Theodore Roosevelt died in his sleep from a blood clot near his heart.

"Death had to take him sleeping," commented Vice President Thomas R. Marshall, "for if Roosevelt had been awake, there would have been a fight."

Chapter 6

The Legacy of Theodore Roosevelt ——

In 1927, eight years after Roosevelt's death, an artist named Gutzon Borglum began an unlikely project in the Black Hills of South Dakota. Using dynamite, he began blasting and sculpting the faces of four great Americans into the rock face of Mount Rushmore. Borglum chose George Washington for his role in founding the new republic; Thomas Jefferson for expanding U.S. territory; and Abraham Lincoln for keeping the country together through the U.S. Civil War.

His fourth choice was Theodore Roosevelt, to represent "the 20th century role of the United States in world affairs and the rights of the common man." It was a bold choice, coming before history had a fair chance to judge Roosevelt's contributions. Yet today it seems a right choice. Most presidential historians agree without hesitation that Roosevelt was a great president, whether or not they agree with his

A portrait of Theodore Roosevelt by the distinguished American painter John Singer Sargent. Sargent reported that Roosevelt was an impatient and difficult subject.

policies and politics. In many ways his leadership ushered in what became known as "the American Century," in which the United States became the world's leading economic and military power.

His presidential legacy falls into four main areas: he expanded the power of the presidency; he created a stronger foreign policy for an emerging world power; he empowered the federal government to regulate the activities of private business; and he promoted protection of the environment and the conservation of natural resources.

Expanding Presidential Power ───────────

Theodore Roosevelt established practices that placed the presidency and the executive branch of government at the heart of national politics. The office of the president had not always been dominant. The U.S. Constitution gave the legislative branch the primary job of considering and passing laws, and allowed the president only the power to veto a law. For generations, the Congress had been at the center of national decision-making.

Roosevelt changed this pattern. By using the power of the president to represent all of the people, he raised the profile of the presidency significantly. He used his skill as a communicator, preaching from what he called the president's "bully pulpit," to influence congressional action. "I did and caused to be done many things not previously done by the President and the heads of the departments," he later reflected. "I did not usurp power, but I did greatly broaden the use of executive power . . . I acted for the common well-being of all our people."

Roosevelt also made full use of the powers given to the president in the Constitution. He believed strongly that the chief executive must have full responsibility for foreign policy, especially in times of crisis. Yet he used this power responsibly. During his years in office, he never risked war, although his critics complained that he bullied weaker nations.

He also found new ways to work around Constitutional limits. He helped mediate the great coal strike even though he had no Constitutional power to intervene, by using the prestige of his office and gaining the grudging trust of both sides. In conservation issues, he pioneered the use of the executive order to bypass Congress, simply announcing the protection of federal lands. "Is there any law that will prevent me from declaring Pelican Island a Federal Bird Reservation?" he asked his advisers. When no one could find such a law, he said, "Very well, then I so declare it!"

Roosevelt's expansion of executive powers is not without its dark side. He was, for the most part, a reasonable and moral leader. Yet critics worried that his example could warp the U.S. political system, giving the presidency too much

Pelican Island in Florida was designated as the nation's first wildlife refuge by President Roosevelt.

power. Even Franklin Roosevelt, another strong president, wondered about his distant cousin's legacy: "The President's tendency to make the executive power stronger than the Houses of Congress is bound to be a bad thing, especially when a man of weaker personality succeeds him in office."

Exercising U.S. Power in the World ————

The economic power of the rapidly growing United States was making it a strong force in the world. Theodore Roosevelt understood this and knew that it must adopt a more forceful foreign policy. He was an interventionist, eager to project U.S. power and prestige beyond U.S. borders. His administration's foreign policy was mostly marked with thoughtful, creative, and courageous diplomacy—with the notable exception of the land grab in Panama.

Roosevelt was a great believer in the importance of a strong military in international relations. He was fond of George Washington's saying: "To be prepared for war is the most effectual means to promote peace." He knew that aggressive foreign powers would be reluctant to attack if the United States was prepared to fight.

Roosevelt especially believed in the value of modern warships. In an era before air power, battleships were the ultimate weapons. During his administra-

A British cartoonist shows Roosevelt as "the world's constable," or policeman. People from Europe (right), Latin America (bottom left), and Asia (center left) complain, but the larger-than-life president keeps the peace with his big stick.

tion, the U.S. Navy rose from the fifth strongest in the world, to second—trailing only Great Britain.

Government Regulation

In 1901, when Roosevelt came to the presidency, giant corporations dominated the country's economy and politics as never before. Few laws protected the public from spoiled food, bad medicine, or unchecked pollution. Few laws protected workers—including children—from unsafe conditions, low wages, and long hours. Few laws prevented businesses from using their power to crush competition, then raise their prices to make huge profits.

Throughout his life, Theodore Roosevelt preached courage and self-reliance. He believed that—all things being equal—individuals made their own luck through hard work and determination. But what if all things *weren't* equal? What if individuals couldn't get a "square deal" from companies or a government agency? Roosevelt met those thorny questions head-on throughout his career in public service.

He agreed that government had a responsibility to protect and encourage business and trade, but he also believed that protecting the average American was vital to peace and prosperity. "We must not only do justice, but be able to show the wage workers that we are doing justice," he wrote in a letter. "The friends of property must realize that the surest way to provoke an explosion of wrong and injustice is to be . . . greedy and arrogant."

As president, he used the courts to break up trusts he felt were taking advantage of the public. He pushed through the Pure Food and Drug Act and the Meat Inspection Act to force those industries to clean up their unsafe practices. He worked for the Hepburn Act to regulate the railroads. He inserted the power of the presidency into labor disputes, often favoring the workers. He argued against child labor and for a woman's right to vote.

Roosevelt created a new model for government activism. During the rest of the century, other leaders would return to this model to provide a "square deal" for everyone.

The Preservationist

Roosevelt's childhood love of nature never left him. As president, he turned his passion for the natural world into policy. He did more for environmental conservation and preservation than any president before or since. During his administration, he quadrupled U.S. land reserves, created 150 national forests and 5 national parks, declared the Grand Canyon and Niagara Falls national monuments, and established 51 wildlife refuges.

The beauty of these undeveloped areas is one of Theodore Roosevelt's most visible and enduring legacies. "The greatest work that Theodore Roosevelt did for the United States," said his friend and pioneer forester Gifford Pinchot, "the great fact which will give his influence vitality and power long after we shall all have gone, is that he changed the attitude of the American people toward conserving the natural resources."

Theodore Roosevelt stands on a promontory overlooking Yosemite Valley with pioneer conservationist John Muir.

American Visionary

If there was ever a national leader who lived life to the fullest, that man was Theodore Roosevelt. He was a true American visionary who believed passionately that government could be an agent for advancing a stronger, fairer, and more intelligent country. "Much has been given us, and much will rightfully be expected from us," he said in his 1905 inaugural address. "We have duties to others and duties to ourselves; and we can shirk neither."

Theodore Roosevelt

Birth:	October 27, 1858
Birthplace:	New York, New York
Parents:	Theodore Roosevelt Sr. and Martha Bulloch Roosevelt
Brothers & Sisters:	Anna "Bamie" Roosevelt Cowles (1855–1931)
	Elliott Roosevelt (1860–1894)
	Corinne Roosevelt Robinson (1861–1933)
Education:	Harvard College, graduated 1880
Occupation:	Author, elected official
Marriage:	To Alice Lee, October 27, 1880, in New York
	To Edith Kermit Carow, December 2, 1886, in London
Children:	(See list in First Lady Fast Facts at right)
Political Parties:	Republican; Progressive
Public Offices:	1882–1884 New York State Assemblyman
	1889–1895 U.S. Civil Service Commissioner
	1895–1897 Police Commissioner of New York City
	1897–1898 Assistant Secretary of the U.S. Navy
	1898–1900 Governor of New York
	1901 Vice President of the United States
	1901–1909 26th President of the United States
His Vice President:	1905–1909 Charles W. Fairbanks
Major Actions as President:	Took legal action against business trusts
	Secured land for Panama Canal
	Established Department of Commerce and Labor
	Built up U.S. Navy
	Set aside millions of acres for conservation of wildlife and natural resources
Firsts:	Visited Panama in 1906; first president to travel to another country while in office
	First American to win Nobel Peace Prize
Death:	January 6, 1919
Age at Death:	60 years
Burial Place:	Young's Memorial Cemetery, Oyster Bay, New York

Edith Kermit Carow Roosevelt

Birth:	August 6, 1861
Birthplace:	Norwich, Connecticut
Parents:	Charles and Gertrude Tyler Carow
Education:	Miss Comstock's School
Marriage:	To Theodore Roosevelt, December 2, 1886, in London
Children:	Alice (1884–1980) (daughter of Alice Lee Roosevelt)
	Theodore Jr. (1887–1944)
	Kermit (1889–1943)
	Ethel (1891–1977)
	Archibald (1894–1979)
	Quentin (1897–1918)
Firsts:	First president's wife to hire a social secretary
	Established tradition of hanging portraits of first ladies in White House
	Oversaw largest renovation of White House in history
Death:	September 30, 1948
Age at Death:	87 years
Burial Place:	Young's Memorial Cemetery, Oyster Bay, New York

Timeline

1858	1861	1878	1880	1882
Theodore Roosevelt Jr. born October 27 in New York City	U.S. Civil War begins; ends in 1865	Father dies of stomach cancer	Graduates from Harvard College with honors; marries Alice Lee	Publishes *The Naval War of 1812*; becomes youngest member of the New York State Assembly

1894	1895	1897	1898	1900
Son Archibald born	Roosevelt becomes president of Police Commission of the City of New York	Appointed Assistant Secretary of the Navy by President McKinley; son Quentin born	Leads the Rough Riders in the Spanish-American War; elected governor of New York	Elected vice president on ticket with President William McKinley

1906	1907	1909	1912	1913
Daughter Alice is married in White House ceremony; Roosevelt signs Pure Food and Drug Act; awarded Nobel Peace Prize	Sends the Great White Fleet on an around-the-world tour	Leaves presidency; succeeded by William Howard Taft; goes hunting in Africa	Presidential nominee of the Progressive party; defeated by Democrat Woodrow Wilson	Publishes his life story, *An Autobiography*; travels to South America

1884	**1886**	**1887**	**1889**	**1891**
Birth of daughter Alice Lee, February 12; wife and mother die February 14; goes to Dakota Territory to ranch	Loses race for mayor of New York City; marries Edith Kermit Carow	Son Theodore Jr. born	Appointed U.S. Civil Service Commissioner; son Kermit born	Daughter Ethel born

1901	**1902**	**1903**	**1904**	**1905**
McKinley shot, September 6; McKinley dies, Roosevelt sworn in as president September 14	Orders antitrust suit against Northern Securities, the first of 45 antitrust suits; settles anthracite coal strike	Recognizes Republic of Panama and signs treaty for Canal Zone; Department of Commerce and Labor established	Elected president by a landslide	Forest Service established; helps negotiate end of Russo-Japanese War

1914	**1917**	**1918**	**1919**
World War I engulfs Europe	U.S. enters the war; five Roosevelt children serve, Ethel as a nurse	Youngest son, Quentin, killed in combat	Dies at Sagamore Hill on January 6

Glossary

anarchist: a person who believes all governments should be abolished

annex: to take control or ownership of a region

arbitration: the negotiation of a dispute in which a neutral person or committee can determine a settlement

cabinet: government department heads who advise the president

civil servants: people who are appointed to jobs in government

discriminate against: to impose unfair restrictions on an individual or a group

executive branch: the part of the federal government that includes the president and the departments that carry out government policy

federal government: the national government, as opposed to state or local governments

natural history: the study of nature

negotiate: to discuss a dispute in order to reach an agreement

reformer: a person eager to make changes to end injustices

strike: to stop work as a way of protesting against an employer

treaty: an official agreement between countries

trust: a related group of businesses governed by the same directors

Further Reading

★ ★ ★ ★ ★

Donnelly, Matt. *Theodore Roosevelt: Larger than Life.* North Haven, CT: Linnet Books, 2003.

Fritz, Jean. *Bully for You, Teddy Roosevelt!* New York: G.P. Putnam's Sons, 1991.

Harness, Cheryl. *Young Teddy Roosevelt.* Washington, DC: National Geographic Society, 1998.

Roosevelt, Theodore. *The Boyhood Diary of Theodore Roosevelt: Early Travels of the 26th U.S. President.* Mankato, MN: Blue Earth Books/Capstone Press, 2001.

Roosevelt, Theodore. *A Bully Father: Theodore Roosevelt's Letters to His Children.* New York: Random House, 1995.

MORE ADVANCED READING

Auchincloss, Louis. *Theodore Roosevelt.* New York: New York Times Books, 2001.

Brands, H. W. *T.R.: The Last Romantic.* New York: Basic Books, 1997.

Gould, Lewis L. *The Presidency of Theodore Roosevelt.* Lawrence: University Press of Kansas, 1991.

May, Ernest R. and the Editors of Time-Life Books. *The Progressive Era.* New York: Time-Life Books, 1980.

Miller, Nathan. *Theodore Roosevelt: A Life.* New York: William Morrow and Company, 1992.

Morris, Edmund. *The Rise of Theodore Roosevelt.* New York: Coward, McCann & Geoghegan, 1979.

Morris, Edmund. *Theodore Rex.* New York: Random House, 2001.

Morris, Sylvia Jukes. *Edith Kermit Roosevelt: Portrait of a First Lady.* New York: Coward, McCann & Geoghegan, 1980.

Roosevelt, Theodore. *An Autobiography.* New York: Da Capo Press, 1985.

Places to Visit

★ ★ ★ ★ ★

Sagamore Hill National Historic Site
20 Sagamore Hill Road
Oyster Bay, NY 11771-1809
(516) 922-4788
http://www.nps.gov/sahi/

Visit the majestic family home of Theodore and Edith Carow Roosevelt, now a museum and national historic site.

Theodore Roosevelt Birthplace
28 East 20th Street
New York, NY 10003
(212) 260-1616
http://www.nps.gov/thrb/

This reconstructed and restored home features books and furnishings from Theodore Roosevelt's childhood.

Theodore Roosevelt National Park
P.O. Box 7
Medora, ND 58645
(701) 623-4466
http://www.nps.gov/thro/

This national park is in the North Dakota Badlands, near the site of Theodore Roosevelt's ranch.

Theodore Roosevelt Inaugural National Historical Site
641 Delaware Avenue
Buffalo, NY 14202
(716) 884-0095
http://www.nps.gov/thri/

The private house, owned by Roosevelt's friend Ansley Wilcox, where Roosevelt was sworn in as president on September 14, 1901, hours after the death of President William McKinley.

Online Sites of Interest

★ **Theodore Roosevelt Association**

http://www.theodoreroosevelt.org/

Excellent source for personal, political, and historical information about Theodore
Roosevelt. Includes many photographs and excerpts from his writings and speeches.

★ **Bartleby**

http://bartleby.com/people/RsvltT.html

Large collection of Theodore Roosevelt's writings.

★ **Internet Public Library, Presidents of the United States (IPL POTUS)**

http://www.ipl.org/div/potus/troosevelt.html

Includes concise information about Roosevelt and his presidency; also provides links to
other sites of interest.

★ **The American President**

http://www.americanpresident.org/history/theodoreroosevelt/

Provides valuable information on the life and times of U.S. presidents. Originally prepared from material for a public television series on the president, the site is now managed by the University of Virginia.

★ **The White House**

http://www.whitehouse.gov/history/presidents/tr26.html

Provides a brief biography of Theodore Roosevelt. The site also provides information
on the current president, biographies of other presidents, and information on timely top-
ics of interest.

★ **The American Presidency**

http://gi.grolier.com/presidents

Provides biographical information on the presidents at different reading levels, based
on material in Scholastic/Grolier encyclopedias.

Table of Presidents

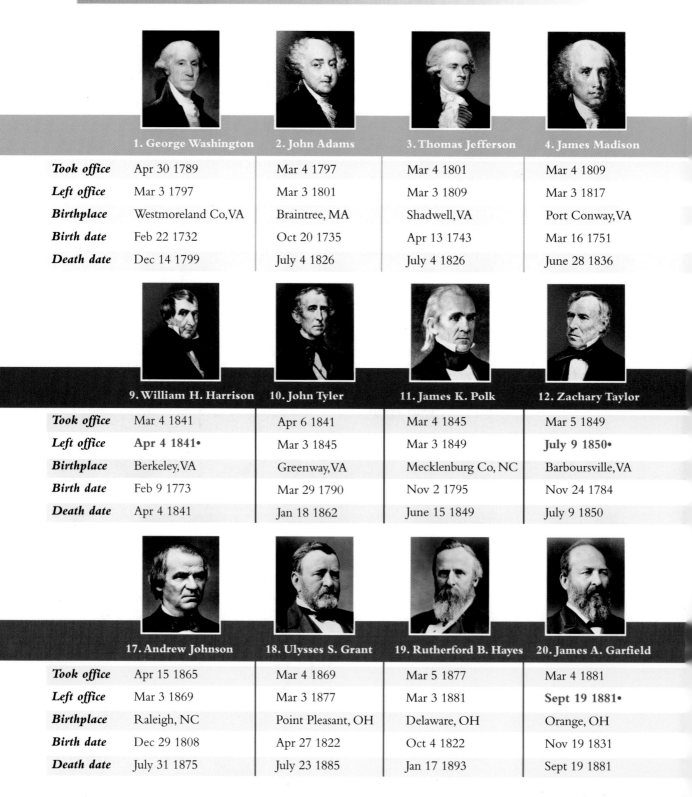

	1. George Washington	2. John Adams	3. Thomas Jefferson	4. James Madison
Took office	Apr 30 1789	Mar 4 1797	Mar 4 1801	Mar 4 1809
Left office	Mar 3 1797	Mar 3 1801	Mar 3 1809	Mar 3 1817
Birthplace	Westmoreland Co, VA	Braintree, MA	Shadwell, VA	Port Conway, VA
Birth date	Feb 22 1732	Oct 20 1735	Apr 13 1743	Mar 16 1751
Death date	Dec 14 1799	July 4 1826	July 4 1826	June 28 1836

	9. William H. Harrison	10. John Tyler	11. James K. Polk	12. Zachary Taylor
Took office	Mar 4 1841	Apr 6 1841	Mar 4 1845	Mar 5 1849
Left office	**Apr 4 1841•**	Mar 3 1845	Mar 3 1849	**July 9 1850•**
Birthplace	Berkeley, VA	Greenway, VA	Mecklenburg Co, NC	Barboursville, VA
Birth date	Feb 9 1773	Mar 29 1790	Nov 2 1795	Nov 24 1784
Death date	Apr 4 1841	Jan 18 1862	June 15 1849	July 9 1850

	17. Andrew Johnson	18. Ulysses S. Grant	19. Rutherford B. Hayes	20. James A. Garfield
Took office	Apr 15 1865	Mar 4 1869	Mar 5 1877	Mar 4 1881
Left office	Mar 3 1869	Mar 3 1877	Mar 3 1881	**Sept 19 1881•**
Birthplace	Raleigh, NC	Point Pleasant, OH	Delaware, OH	Orange, OH
Birth date	Dec 29 1808	Apr 27 1822	Oct 4 1822	Nov 19 1831
Death date	July 31 1875	July 23 1885	Jan 17 1893	Sept 19 1881

5. James Monroe

Mar 4 1817

Mar 3 1825

Westmoreland Co, VA

Apr 28 1758

July 4 1831

6. John Quincy Adams

Mar 4 1825

Mar 3 1829

Braintree, MA

July 11 1767

Feb 23 1848

7. Andrew Jackson

Mar 4 1829

Mar 3 1837

The Waxhaws, SC

Mar 15 1767

June 8 1845

8. Martin Van Buren

Mar 4 1837

Mar 3 1841

Kinderhook, NY

Dec 5 1782

July 24 1862

13. Millard Fillmore

July 9 1850

Mar 3 1853

Locke Township, NY

Jan 7 1800

Mar 8 1874

14. Franklin Pierce

Mar 4 1853

Mar 3 1857

Hillsborough, NH

Nov 23 1804

Oct 8 1869

15. James Buchanan

Mar 4 1857

Mar 3 1861

Cove Gap, PA

Apr 23 1791

June 1 1868

16. Abraham Lincoln

Mar 4 1861

Apr 15 1865•

Hardin Co, KY

Feb 12 1809

Apr 15 1865

21. Chester A. Arthur

Sept 19 1881

Mar 3 1885

Fairfield, VT

Oct 5 1829

Nov 18 1886

22. Grover Cleveland

Mar 4 1885

Mar 3 1889

Caldwell, NJ

Mar 18 1837

June 24 1908

23. Benjamin Harrison

Mar 4 1889

Mar 3 1893

North Bend, OH

Aug 20 1833

Mar 13 1901

24. Grover Cleveland

Mar 4 1893

Mar 3 1897

Caldwell, NJ

Mar 18 1837

June 24 1908

25. William McKinley | **26. Theodore Roosevelt** | **27. William H. Taft** | **28. Woodrow Wilson**

	25. William McKinley	26. Theodore Roosevelt	27. William H. Taft	28. Woodrow Wilson
Took office	Mar 4 1897	Sept 14 1901	Mar 4 1909	Mar 4 1913
Left office	**Sept 14 1901**•	Mar 3 1909	Mar 3 1913	Mar 3 1921
Birthplace	Niles, OH	New York, NY	Cincinnati, OH	Staunton, VA
Birth date	Jan 29 1843	Oct 27 1858	Sept 15 1857	Dec 28 1856
Death date	Sept 14 1901	Jan 6 1919	Mar 8 1930	Feb 3 1924

	33. Harry S. Truman	34. Dwight D. Eisenhower	35. John F. Kennedy	36. Lyndon B. Johnson
Took office	Apr 12 1945	Jan 20 1953	Jan 20 1961	Nov 22 1963
Left office	Jan 20 1953	Jan 20 1961	**Nov 22 1963**•	Jan 20 1969
Birthplace	Lamar, MO	Denison, TX	Brookline, MA	Johnson City, TX
Birth date	May 8 1884	Oct 14 1890	May 29 1917	Aug 27 1908
Death date	Dec 26 1972	Mar 28 1969	Nov 22 1963	Jan 22 1973

	41. George Bush	42. Bill Clinton	43. George W. Bush	
Took office	Jan 20 1989	Jan 20 1993	Jan 20 2001	
Left office	Jan 20 1993	Jan 20 2001	—	
Birthplace	Milton, MA	Hope, AR	New Haven, CT	
Birth date	June 12 1924	Aug 19 1946	July 6 1946	
Death date	—	—	—	

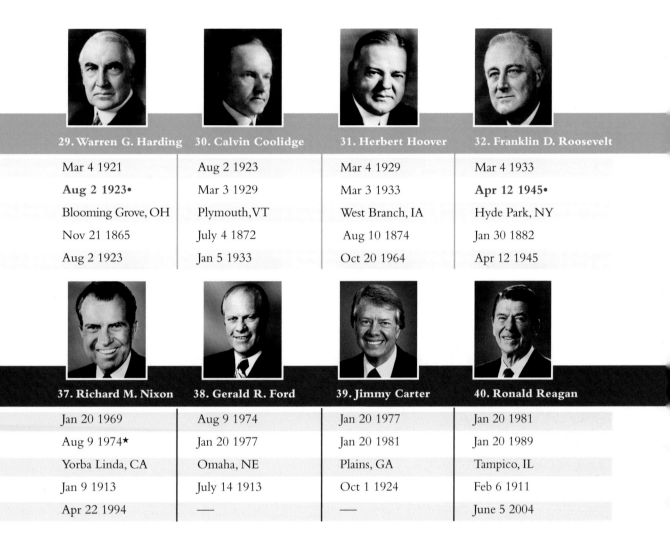

29. Warren G. Harding	30. Calvin Coolidge	31. Herbert Hoover	32. Franklin D. Roosevelt
Mar 4 1921	Aug 2 1923	Mar 4 1929	Mar 4 1933
Aug 2 1923•	Mar 3 1929	Mar 3 1933	**Apr 12 1945•**
Blooming Grove, OH	Plymouth, VT	West Branch, IA	Hyde Park, NY
Nov 21 1865	July 4 1872	Aug 10 1874	Jan 30 1882
Aug 2 1923	Jan 5 1933	Oct 20 1964	Apr 12 1945

37. Richard M. Nixon	38. Gerald R. Ford	39. Jimmy Carter	40. Ronald Reagan
Jan 20 1969	Aug 9 1974	Jan 20 1977	Jan 20 1981
Aug 9 1974★	Jan 20 1977	Jan 20 1981	Jan 20 1989
Yorba Linda, CA	Omaha, NE	Plains, GA	Tampico, IL
Jan 9 1913	July 14 1913	Oct 1 1924	Feb 6 1911
Apr 22 1994	—	—	June 5 2004

• Indicates the president died while in office.

★ Richard Nixon resigned before his term expired.

Index

★ ★ ★ ★ ★

Page numbers in *italics* indicate illustrations.

About the Author

Theodore Roosevelt loved life and adventure, and that attitude rings throughout his history and writings. Author Sean McCollum found that the greatest challenge was picking the very best of hundreds of entertaining and revealing stories about the 26th U.S. president so that the book didn't run way too long.

Sean loves writing for middle-grade readers and learning along with them. He has written about three other presidents for this series—John Quincy Adams, James K. Polk, and Bill Clinton—and published 12 other books. He is also a regular contributor to *Boys' Life*, *Junior Scholastic*, and *National Geographic Kids*. He has been lost in more than 40 countries, but lives near the Colorado Rocky Mountains.